# Fundamentals of
# Edge Computing

L HALDURAI

V JANANI PRARTHANA

Made with ♥ on the Notion Press Platform

www.notionpress.com

# About the Authors

Mr.L. Haldurai, is working as an Assistant Professor in the Department of Computer Science (Artificial Intelligence & Data Science) at Sri Ramakrishna College of Arts and Science, Coimbatore. He has completed MCA, M.Phil, M.Sc (App.Psy), B.Ed, NET., His research areas are Data mining, Artificial Intelligence and Machine Learning. He has published 3 Books, 11 International Journals, 2 Patents, 1 Book chapters and attended various Workshops and FDPs. He has 16 years of Teaching Experience.

Ms.V. Janani Prarthana, is working as an Assistant Professor in the Department of Computer Applications at Kongunadu Arts and Science College, Coimbatore. She pursued her under graduation and Post-graduation in Kongunadu Arts and Science College. She has published a book chapter and also published paper in International Conference proceedings. Her research area is Data mining.

# 1. INTRODUCTION TO EDGE COMPUTING

## 1.1 Definition and Conceptual Overview

In the context of computing, edge computing refers to a decentralized approach to data processing, where computational tasks are performed closer to the data source or the "edge" of the network, rather than relying solely on centralized data centres or cloud servers. This paradigm shift is driven by the increasing volume of data generated by devices and sensors at the periphery of networks, such as IoT devices, mobile phones, and industrial equipment.

At its core, edge computing aims to reduce latency, enhance efficiency, and improve scalability by processing data closer to where it is generated or consumed. Instead of sending all data to a centralized data center or cloud for processing and analysis, edge computing distributes these tasks across a network of local devices, servers, and gateways.

Conceptually, edge computing can be envisioned as a continuum that spans from the cloud to the edge, with varying levels of computational power and proximity to the data source. At one end of the spectrum, you have traditional cloud computing, which offers vast storage and computational resources but may introduce latency and bandwidth constraints, especially for real-time applications. At the other end, you have edge devices and sensors that are directly embedded within the physical environment, capable of processing data on-site with minimal latency.

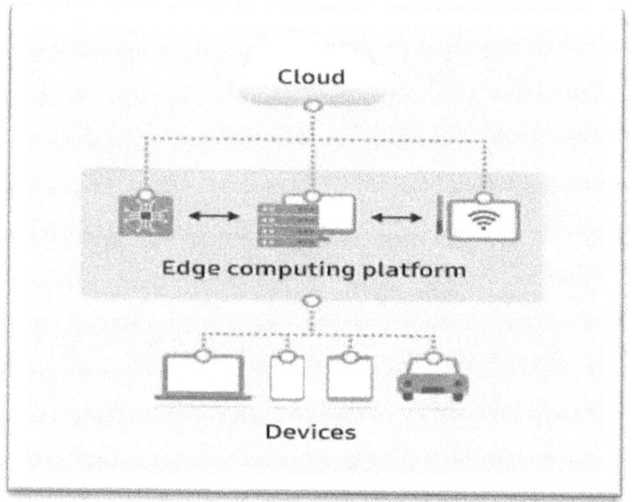


Fig.1 Edge Computing

***Key aspects of edge computing include:***

**Proximity:** Edge computing places computational resources closer to where data is generated, reducing the distance data needs to travel and therefore minimizing latency.

**Distributed Processing:** Rather than relying on a centralized server or data center, edge computing distributes computational tasks across a network of edge devices, gateways, and servers.

**Real-time Processing:** Edge computing enables real-time or near-real-time processing of data, making it ideal for applications that require low latency, such as autonomous vehicles, industrial automation, and augmented reality.

**Scalability:** By distributing computational tasks across multiple edge nodes, edge computing offers scalability and flexibility to adapt to changing demands and accommodate growing volumes of data.

**Efficiency:** Edge computing can optimize bandwidth usage and reduce data transfer costs by filtering and processing data locally before sending only relevant information to the cloud.

Overall, edge computing represents a shift towards a more distributed, decentralized computing paradigm, offering a new approach to meet the evolving requirements of modern applications and services in an increasingly interconnected world.

## 1.2 Evolution from Cloud Computing

The evolution from cloud computing to edge computing represents a natural progression driven by the changing landscape of technology requirements and advancements in computing infrastructure. Here's a breakdown of this evolution:

**Centralized Cloud Computing:** Cloud computing emerged as a paradigm shift from traditional on-premises infrastructure to centralized data centers, where computing resources such as servers, storage, and networking are provided as a service over the internet. This centralized model offered scalability, flexibility, and cost-efficiency, enabling organizations to offload their IT operations and focus on core business activities.

**Rise of IoT and Data Deluge:** The proliferation of connected devices, sensors, and IoT (Internet of Things) technology led to an explosion of data generation at the network edge. These devices generate vast amounts of data in real-time, often requiring immediate processing and analysis to derive actionable insights. Sending all this data to centralized cloud servers for processing introduces latency, bandwidth constraints, and privacy concerns.

**Latency-sensitive Applications:** With the increasing demand for latency-sensitive applications such as autonomous vehicles, industrial automation, augmented reality, and telemedicine, the limitations of centralized cloud computing became more apparent. These applications require real-time or near-real-time processing of data, which is challenging to achieve with traditional cloud architectures due to network latency and bandwidth limitations.

**Need for Edge Computing:** Edge computing emerged as a solution to address the shortcomings of centralized cloud computing for latency-sensitive and bandwidth-intensive applications. By moving computation closer to the data source or "edge" of the network, edge computing reduces latency, improves responsiveness, and enhances the overall user experience. It enables localized data processing, analysis, and decision-making, while still leveraging the scalability and resources of the cloud when needed.

**Hybrid Cloud-Edge Architectures:** Recognizing the complementary nature of cloud and edge computing, organizations are increasingly adopting hybrid architectures that combine the strengths of both paradigms. In a hybrid cloud-edge architecture, critical tasks are performed at the edge for low-latency processing, while non-latency-sensitive or resource-intensive tasks are offloaded to centralized cloud servers for scalability and analytics.

**Edge-to-Cloud Continuum:** The evolution from cloud computing to edge computing has led to the emergence of an edge-to-cloud continuum, where data processing and storage are distributed across a spectrum of edge devices, gateways, edge servers, and centralized cloud infrastructure. This continuum allows organizations to dynamically allocate resources based on workload requirements, optimize performance, and ensure data sovereignty and compliance.

Overall, the evolution from cloud computing to edge computing reflects a shift towards a more distributed, decentralized computing paradigm, driven by the need for real-time responsiveness, scalability, and efficiency in an increasingly connected world.

## 1.3 Motivation and Benefits

The motivation behind adopting edge computing lies in addressing the limitations of traditional centralized computing architectures, such as cloud computing, and leveraging the benefits offered by distributing computational tasks closer to the data source or the "edge" of the network.

Here are some key motivations and benefits of edge computing:

**Reduced Latency:** Edge computing minimizes the time it takes for data to travel between the source and the processing point by performing computations closer to where data is generated. This reduces latency, enabling real-time or near-real-time responsiveness for latency-sensitive applications such as autonomous vehicles, industrial automation, and augmented reality.

**Improved Performance:** By distributing computational tasks across a network of edge devices, gateways, and servers, edge computing can improve overall system performance and efficiency. This allows for faster data processing, analysis, and decision-making, leading to enhanced user experiences and better application performance.

**Bandwidth Optimization:** Edge computing helps optimize bandwidth usage by processing and filtering data locally before sending only relevant information to centralized cloud servers for further analysis or storage. This reduces the amount of data transmitted over the network, minimizing bandwidth costs and alleviating network congestion.

**Data Privacy and Compliance:** Edge computing enables organizations to keep sensitive data local and comply with data privacy regulations and compliance requirements. By processing data locally at the edge, organizations can ensure data sovereignty, minimize the risk of data breaches, and address privacy concerns associated with transmitting sensitive information over the network.

**Resilience and Reliability:** Edge computing enhances system resilience and reliability by reducing dependency on centralized cloud infrastructure. In edge environments, even if connectivity to the cloud is lost, local devices and servers can continue to operate autonomously, ensuring uninterrupted service delivery and business continuity.

**Scalability and Flexibility:** Edge computing offers scalability and flexibility to adapt to changing demands and accommodate growing volumes of data. Edge nodes can be easily deployed and scaled out to meet specific workload requirements, allowing organizations to dynamically allocate resources based on demand and optimize resource utilization.

**Cost-Efficiency:** Edge computing can help reduce operational costs associated with data transfer, storage, and processing by leveraging local resources more efficiently. By offloading computational tasks to edge devices and minimizing reliance on centralized cloud infrastructure, organizations can optimize resource usage and reduce cloud service costs.

**Support for Emerging Technologies:** Edge computing provides a platform for deploying and supporting emerging technologies such as artificial intelligence (AI), machine learning (ML), and Internet of Things (IoT) applications. By bringing computation closer to the data source, edge computing enables real-time analytics, predictive maintenance, and intelligent decision-making at the edge of the network.

Overall, the motivation and benefits of edge computing stem from its ability to improve performance, reduce latency, enhance data privacy and compliance, increase resilience, and support the scalability and flexibility required to meet the evolving requirements of modern applications and services in an interconnected world.

## 1.4 Use Cases and Applications

Edge computing has a wide range of applications across various industries, leveraging its ability to process data closer to the source and deliver real-time or near-real-time insights. Here are some prominent use cases and applications of edge computing:

**Internet of Things (IoT):**

➢ Smart Home Automation: Edge computing enables smart home devices such as thermostats, cameras, and sensors to process data locally, improving responsiveness and privacy.

➢ Industrial IoT (IIoT): Edge computing supports real-time monitoring and control of industrial equipment, predictive maintenance, and process optimization in manufacturing and logistics.

**Autonomous Vehicles:**

➢ Connected Cars: Edge computing enables autonomous vehicles to process sensor data in real-time for navigation, object detection, collision avoidance, and decision-making, enhancing safety and reliability.

> Vehicle-to-Everything (V2X): Edge computing facilitates vehicle-to-vehicle (V2V) and vehicle-to-infrastructure (V2I) communication for traffic management, congestion prediction, and cooperative driving.

**Smart Cities:**

> Traffic Management: Edge computing supports intelligent traffic signal control, congestion detection, and predictive analytics to optimize traffic flow and reduce commute times.

> Public Safety: Edge-enabled video surveillance, gunshot detection, and emergency response systems enhance public safety and security in urban environments.

**Healthcare:**

> Telemedicine: Edge computing enables remote patient monitoring, real-time health data analysis,

and teleconsultation, improving access to healthcare services and patient outcomes.

> Wearable Health Devices: Edge computing supports wearable devices such as fitness trackers and smartwatches to monitor vital signs, detect anomalies, and provide personalized health insights.

**Retail:**

> Personalized Marketing: Edge computing enables retailers to analyze customer behavior in-store, deliver targeted promotions, and enhance the shopping experience through interactive displays and digital signage.

> Inventory Management: Edge-enabled sensors and RFID tags provide real-time inventory visibility, optimize stock levels, and reduce out-of-stock situations.

**Energy Management:**

> Smart Grids: Edge computing supports intelligent energy distribution, demand response, and predictive maintenance in smart grid infrastructures, improving efficiency and reliability.

➢ Renewable Energy Integration: Edge-enabled monitoring and control systems optimize the integration of renewable energy sources such as solar and wind power into the grid, maximizing utilization and minimizing wastage.

**Edge Gaming and Entertainment:**

➢ Cloud Gaming: Edge computing reduces latency in cloud gaming platforms, enabling seamless streaming and immersive gaming experiences.

➢ Augmented Reality (AR) and Virtual Reality (VR): Edge computing supports real-time rendering, spatial mapping, and content delivery for AR and VR applications, enhancing immersion and interactivity.

**Remote Monitoring and Maintenance:**

➢ Asset Tracking: Edge computing enables real-time tracking and monitoring of assets such as vehicles, equipment, and inventory, improving visibility and security.

➢ Predictive Maintenance: Edge analytics predict equipment failures, schedule maintenance activities, and optimize resource allocation, reducing downtime and maintenance costs.

These use cases demonstrate the versatility and potential impact of edge computing across various domains, enabling organizations to leverage real-time insights, improve operational efficiency, and enhance user experiences in an increasingly connected world.

## 1.5 Challenges and Limitations

While edge computing offers numerous benefits and opportunities, it also presents several challenges and limitations that organizations need to address. Here are some key challenges and limitations of edge computing:

**Resource Constraints:**

➢ Limited Processing Power: Edge devices often have limited computational capabilities compared to centralized cloud servers, which can constrain the types and complexity of tasks that can be performed at the edge.

➢ Restricted Storage: Edge devices may have limited storage capacity, restricting the amount of data that can be stored locally for processing and analysis.

**Network Connectivity:**

➢ Intermittent Connectivity: Edge devices may operate in environments with intermittent or unreliable network connectivity, which can disrupt communication with centralized systems and affect data synchronization and updates.

➢ Bandwidth Limitations: Limited bandwidth in edge environments may restrict the amount of data that can be transmitted between edge devices and centralized cloud servers, impacting real-time communication and data transfer.

**Data Security and Privacy:**

➢ Data Exposure: Edge devices may store and process sensitive data locally, increasing the risk of data exposure and unauthorized access if adequate security measures are not implemented.

➢ Data Governance: Ensuring compliance with data privacy regulations and governance policies becomes challenging when data is distributed across a network of edge devices and centralized cloud servers.

**Management Complexity:**

> ➢ Distributed Infrastructure: Managing a distributed edge infrastructure comprising numerous devices, gateways, and servers can be complex and challenging, requiring robust orchestration, monitoring, and management tools.

> ➢ Software Updates and Maintenance: Updating and maintaining software and firmware across a heterogeneous edge environment can be cumbersome and time-consuming, increasing operational overhead.

**Application Portability and Compatibility:**

> ➢ Platform Heterogeneity: Edge environments may consist of diverse hardware platforms, operating systems, and software stacks, leading to compatibility issues and portability challenges for edge applications.

> ➢ Vendor Lock-in: Organizations may face vendor lock-in when deploying edge solutions that rely on proprietary technologies or vendor-specific ecosystems, limiting flexibility and interoperability.

**Scalability and Performance:**

> Scaling Challenges: Scaling edge deployments to accommodate increasing workloads and data volumes while maintaining performance and responsiveness can be challenging, especially in dynamic or resource-constrained environments.

> Performance Variability: Performance may vary across edge devices and locations due to differences in hardware capabilities, network conditions, and environmental factors, affecting application consistency and user experience.

**Edge-to-Cloud Integration:**

> Data Consistency: Ensuring data consistency and synchronization between edge devices and centralized cloud servers becomes critical in hybrid edge-to-cloud architectures, requiring efficient data replication and synchronization mechanisms.

> Service Orchestration: Orchestrating services and workloads across edge and cloud environments to optimize resource usage, minimize latency, and ensure scalability poses integration and management challenges.

Addressing these challenges and limitations requires a holistic approach that combines technical innovation, operational excellence, and collaboration across stakeholders. Organizations must carefully evaluate their use cases, infrastructure requirements, and risk profiles to effectively harness the benefits of edge computing while mitigating associated challenges.

# 2. ARCHITECTURES AND TECHNOLOGIES

## 2.1 Edge infrastructure components

Edge infrastructure components are the fundamental building blocks that constitute the distributed architecture of edge computing. These components play crucial roles in enabling data processing, analysis, and decision-making closer to the source of data generation. Here are the key edge infrastructure components:

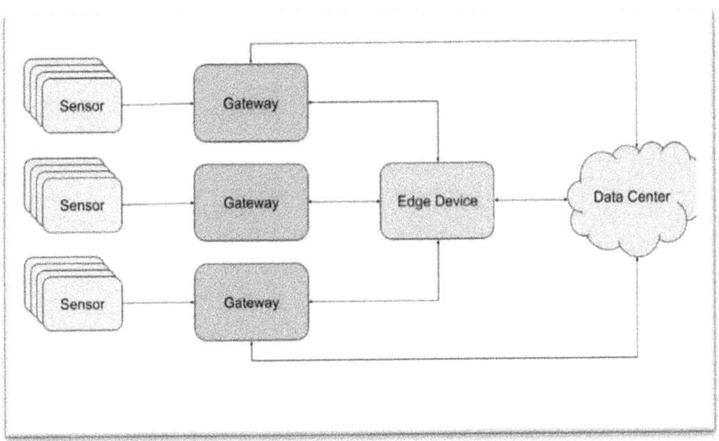


Fig 1. Edge infrastructure components

## *Edge Devices:*

**Sensors:** Sensors are devices that detect and measure physical phenomena such as temperature, pressure, motion, light, and sound. They serve as the primary data sources in edge computing environments, capturing real-world events and generating raw sensor data.

**Actuators:** Actuators are devices that convert electrical signals into physical actions, such as motors, valves, and relays. They enable control and automation in edge applications by responding to commands and triggering physical responses based on processed data.

*Edge Gateways:*

**Data Aggregation:** Edge gateways aggregate data from multiple edge devices and sensors, acting as data hubs or intermediaries between edge devices and centralized cloud infrastructure.

**Preprocessing:** Gateways preprocess and filter raw sensor data to reduce noise, extract relevant information, and perform initial data cleansing before transmitting it to the cloud or edge servers.

**Protocol Translation:** Gateways support various communication protocols and standards to facilitate interoperability between heterogeneous edge devices, enabling seamless data exchange and integration.

**Edge Intelligence:** Some edge gateways incorporate computational capabilities to perform edge analytics, machine learning inference, or decision-making locally, enabling real-time insights and autonomous operation at the edge.

### *Edge Servers:*

**Processing Power:** Edge servers provide computational resources for processing, analyzing, and storing data locally, closer to the source of data generation. They offer higher processing power, memory, and storage capacity compared to edge devices, enabling more complex computations and analytics.

**Application Hosting:** Edge servers host edge applications, services, and workloads that require real-time or near-real-time processing, such as predictive maintenance, anomaly detection, and video analytics.

**Low-Latency Communication:** Edge servers facilitate low-latency communication and interaction between edge devices and centralized cloud infrastructure, supporting applications that require rapid response times and minimal latency.

**Edge-to-Cloud Integration:** Edge servers act as gateways for transmitting processed data to centralized cloud servers for further analysis, storage, or archival, enabling seamless integration between edge and cloud environments.

***Edge Data Centers:***

**Regional Presence:** Edge data centers are geographically distributed facilities located closer to end-users or edge computing deployments, reducing latency and improving performance for local applications and services.

**Scalability:** Edge data centers offer scalability and flexibility to accommodate growing volumes of edge computing workloads, supporting dynamic resource allocation and workload management.

**Resilience:** Edge data centers enhance system resilience and reliability by providing redundant infrastructure, backup power, and disaster recovery capabilities to ensure uninterrupted operation and data availability in case of failures or outages.

***Networking Infrastructure:***

**Edge Networks:** Edge networks comprise wired and wireless communication infrastructure that connects edge devices, gateways, servers, and data centers. They provide high-speed, low-latency connectivity for data transmission and communication between distributed components.

**Edge Routers and Switches:** Edge routers and switches manage network traffic, route data packets, and ensure efficient communication between edge devices and servers. They optimize network performance and reliability in edge environments, supporting Quality of Service (QoS) and traffic prioritization.

**Edge Protocols:** Edge protocols such as MQTT, CoAP, AMQP, and HTTP/HTTPS facilitate communication and data exchange between edge devices, gateways, and servers, ensuring interoperability and compatibility in heterogeneous environments.

By understanding and leveraging these edge infrastructure components, organizations can design, deploy, and manage edge computing solutions that meet their specific requirements for performance, scalability, reliability, and efficiency in diverse use cases and applications.

## 2.2 Fog Computing vs. Edge Computing

Fog computing and edge computing are both distributed computing paradigms that aim to bring computational resources closer to the source of data generation. While they share similar objectives, they have distinct characteristics and architectural differences. Here's a comparison between fog computing and edge computing:

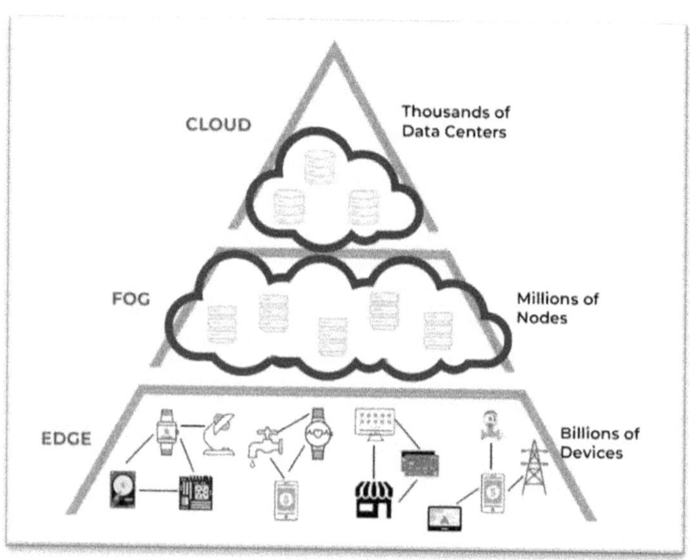


Fig 2. Cloud vs Fog vs Edge Computing

### *Fog Computing:*

**Definition:** Fog computing extends cloud computing capabilities to the edge of the network, closer to the data source. It involves deploying computational resources, storage, and applications at the network edge, typically within the local area network (LAN) or on the premises of the organization.

**Location:** Fog computing resources are typically deployed at the network edge, which can include edge devices, routers, switches, access points, and local servers. Fog nodes are strategically placed in proximity to where data is generated to minimize latency and optimize data processing.

**Hierarchy:** Fog computing introduces a hierarchical architecture with multiple layers of fog nodes, ranging from the cloud to the edge. This hierarchy enables data processing and analysis to occur at different levels of the network, allowing for localized decision-making and resource optimization.

**Scalability:** Fog computing supports scalability and flexibility by distributing computational tasks across multiple fog nodes within the network. This allows organizations to dynamically allocate resources based on workload requirements and scale out edge deployments as needed.

**Applications:** Fog computing is well-suited for applications that require low-latency data processing, real-time analytics, and distributed decision-making in distributed IoT, industrial automation, smart cities, and telecommunications.

### *Edge Computing:*

**Definition:** Edge computing brings computational resources directly to the edge devices, sensors, and endpoints where data is generated. It focuses on processing data locally at the point of origin, without necessarily involving intermediate fog nodes or cloud servers.

**Location:** Edge computing resources are deployed directly on or near the edge devices, sensors, and endpoints where data is generated. Edge servers or gateways may be deployed in close proximity to the source of data to minimize latency and optimize data processing.

**Decentralization:** Edge computing emphasizes a decentralized architecture with a distributed network of edge devices and servers. Each edge device or server operates autonomously and performs local data processing, analysis, and decision-making without relying on centralized infrastructure.

**Resource Constraints:** Edge devices often have limited computational resources, memory, and storage capacity compared to fog nodes or cloud servers. This constraint influences the types of tasks and applications that can be deployed at the edge and requires optimization for resource efficiency.

**Applications:** Edge computing is particularly suitable for applications that require real-time or near-real-time processing, low-latency communication, and autonomy at the edge. Examples include autonomous vehicles, smart appliances, wearable devices, and remote monitoring systems.

In summary, while both fog computing and edge computing aim to distribute computational resources closer to the data source, they differ in their architectural approach, location of deployment, scalability characteristics, and suitability for various applications. Fog computing emphasizes a hierarchical architecture with distributed fog nodes across the network edge, while edge computing focuses on decentralized processing directly at the edge devices and endpoints. Both paradigms play important roles in enabling efficient, scalable, and responsive distributed computing infrastructures for the Internet of Things (IoT) and other emerging applications.

## 2.3 Hardware Considerations:

Hardware considerations are crucial in designing and deploying effective edge computing solutions. Each component—edge devices, gateways, and servers—plays a specific role in enabling distributed computing closer to the data source. Here's a breakdown of hardware considerations for each component:

## 1. Edge Devices:

**Processing Power:** Edge devices vary in their computational capabilities, ranging from low-power microcontrollers to powerful multi-core processors. The choice of processing power depends on the complexity of tasks to be performed at the edge and the available energy budget.

**Memory:** Edge devices require sufficient memory (RAM) to store and manipulate data during processing. The amount of memory needed depends on the size of datasets, computational algorithms, and software applications running on the device.

**Storage:** Edge devices may need local storage (e.g., flash memory or SSDs) to store data, firmware, and application code. The storage capacity required depends on the volume of data to be stored locally and the duration of storage.

**Connectivity:** Edge devices may require various communication interfaces such as Ethernet, Wi-Fi, Bluetooth, Zigbee, LoRa, or cellular connectivity (e.g., 4G/5G) to communicate with other devices, gateways, and servers. The choice of connectivity depends on factors such as range, bandwidth, power consumption, and environmental conditions.

**Power Supply:** Edge devices may operate on battery power or external power sources. Power-efficient designs, low-power standby modes, and energy harvesting techniques can help extend battery life and reduce power consumption.

**2. Gateways:**

**Processing Capabilities:** Gateways act as intermediaries between edge devices and servers, performing data aggregation, preprocessing, and filtering tasks. They require sufficient processing power to handle data from multiple edge devices simultaneously and execute edge analytics algorithms.

**Connectivity:** Gateways need multiple communication interfaces to connect to edge devices, servers, and the internet. This includes wired interfaces (Ethernet) and wireless interfaces (Wi-Fi, cellular, Bluetooth) to support various communication protocols and standards.

**Memory and Storage:** Gateways require memory (RAM) to buffer incoming data and store intermediate results during preprocessing. They also need local storage (e.g., SSDs or HDDs) to cache data, firmware, and software updates.

**Security Features:** Gateways should include security features such as hardware-based encryption, secure boot, and tamper-resistant designs to protect against cyber threats and unauthorized access to data.

**Reliability and Redundancy:** Gateways may incorporate redundant components (e.g., power supplies, network interfaces) and fault-tolerant designs to ensure high availability and reliability in mission-critical applications.

**3. Servers:**

**Processing Power:** Edge servers provide computational resources for processing, analyzing, and storing data locally. They require high-performance processors (e.g., multi-core CPUs, GPUs, FPGAs) to handle intensive data processing tasks, machine learning algorithms, and real-time analytics.

**Memory and Storage:** Edge servers need ample memory (RAM) to support in-memory processing, caching, and buffering of data. They also require large storage capacities (e.g., SSDs, HDDs, or NVMe drives) to store datasets, application code, and historical data.

**Networking Interfaces:** Edge servers should have multiple network interfaces (e.g., Ethernet, 10GbE, or fiber-optic connections) to support high-speed data transfer and communication with other servers, gateways, and cloud infrastructure.

**Scalability:** Edge servers should be scalable to accommodate growing workloads and data volumes. This may involve modular designs, blade servers, or hyper-converged infrastructure (HCI) architectures that allow for easy expansion and resource allocation.

**Reliability and Redundancy:** Edge servers may incorporate redundant components, hot-swappable drives, and RAID configurations to ensure high availability, fault tolerance, and data resilience in edge computing deployments.

By considering these hardware considerations for edge devices, gateways, and servers, organizations can design and deploy robust, scalable, and efficient edge computing solutions that meet their specific requirements for performance, reliability, and functionality in diverse applications and use cases.

## 2.4 Software Considerations:

Software considerations are critical in designing and implementing edge computing solutions, encompassing edge platforms and operating systems tailored to the unique requirements of distributed computing at the edge. Here's an overview of software considerations for edge platforms and operating systems:

## 1. Edge Platforms:

**Definition:** Edge platforms provide the software framework and infrastructure for deploying, managing, and orchestrating edge applications and services. They abstract the underlying hardware complexity and provide a unified interface for developers to build, deploy, and monitor edge workloads.

**Features:**

**Containerization:** Edge platforms leverage containerization technologies (e.g., Docker, Kubernetes) to package edge applications and their dependencies into lightweight, portable containers. Containers enable consistency, portability, and isolation for edge workloads across diverse edge environments.

**Orchestration:** Edge platforms offer orchestration capabilities to manage the lifecycle of edge applications, including deployment, scaling, monitoring, and fault recovery. Orchestration ensures efficient resource utilization, workload distribution, and high availability in distributed edge deployments.

**Edge Analytics:** Some edge platforms incorporate edge analytics capabilities to perform real-time data processing, machine learning inference, and decision-making directly at the edge. Edge analytics enables insights generation, anomaly detection, and autonomous operation in latency-sensitive applications.

**Security:** Edge platforms provide security features such as authentication, authorization, encryption, and secure communication protocols to protect edge applications and data from cyber threats and unauthorized access. Security is paramount in edge computing deployments, especially in mission-critical applications.

**Edge-to-Cloud Integration:** Edge platforms facilitate seamless integration between edge and cloud environments, enabling data synchronization, workload migration, and hybrid edge-cloud architectures. They provide APIs, SDKs, and connectors for interoperability and data exchange between distributed components.

**Examples:**

**AWS IoT Greengrass**: Amazon Web Services (AWS) IoT Greengrass extends AWS cloud capabilities to edge devices, enabling local execution of AWS Lambda functions, machine learning inference, and device shadow synchronization.

**Microsoft Azure IoT Edge**: Azure IoT Edge extends Azure cloud services to edge devices, allowing deployment of containerized workloads, AI models, and custom modules for real-time analytics and processing at the edge.

**Google Cloud IoT Edge:** Google Cloud IoT Edge provides tools and services for deploying, managing, and scaling edge workloads on Google Cloud Platform (GCP). It supports containerization, orchestration, and integration with GCP services for edge-to-cloud data flow.

## 2. Operating Systems (OS):

**Definition:** Edge operating systems are lightweight, optimized operating systems designed for edge devices, gateways, and servers. They provide the foundation for running edge applications, managing hardware resources, and facilitating communication between components.

**Features:**

**Resource Efficiency:** Edge OSs are designed to be resource-efficient, with minimal memory and CPU overhead, to run effectively on resource-constrained edge devices. They prioritize performance, responsiveness, and low latency for edge applications.

**Real-Time Capabilities:** Some edge OSs offer real-time capabilities to support deterministic behavior, predictable response times, and critical task scheduling in time-sensitive applications such as industrial automation and robotics.

**Security:** Edge OSs incorporate security features such as secure boot, trusted execution environments (TEEs), and hardware-based encryption to protect against cyber threats, malware, and unauthorized access to edge devices and data.

**Connectivity:** Edge OSs provide support for various communication protocols and standards to facilitate seamless connectivity with edge devices, gateways, servers, and cloud infrastructure. They ensure interoperability and compatibility in heterogeneous edge environments.

**Manageability:** Edge OSs include management tools, remote administration capabilities, and over-the-air (OTA) update mechanisms to simplify deployment, configuration, and maintenance of edge devices and servers at scale.

**Examples:**

**Linux-based distributions:** Lightweight Linux distributions such as Ubuntu Core, CentOS IoT, and Raspbian are popular choices for edge devices and gateways due to their flexibility, modularity, and extensive software ecosystem.

**Real-time Operating Systems (RTOS):** RTOSs such as FreeRTOS, Zephyr, and NuttX are optimized for embedded systems and IoT devices, offering deterministic behavior, low latency, and minimal overhead for time-critical applications.

**Containerized Platforms:** Containerized platforms such as BalenaOS and ResinOS enable containerized edge applications to run efficiently on edge devices, providing isolation, portability, and scalability for edge workloads.

By considering these software considerations for edge platforms and operating systems, organizations can build, deploy, and manage resilient, scalable, and secure edge computing solutions that meet their specific requirements for performance, reliability, and flexibility in diverse edge environments.

## 2.5 Networking Technologies:

Networking technologies play a crucial role in enabling communication and data exchange between edge devices, gateways, servers, and centralized cloud infrastructure in edge computing deployments. Here's an overview of key networking technologies relevant to edge computing:

## 1. IoT Protocols:

**MQTT (Message Queuing Telemetry Transport):** MQTT is a lightweight publish-subscribe messaging protocol designed for constrained devices and low-bandwidth, high-latency networks. It is commonly used in IoT applications for efficient data transmission, device-to-device communication, and telemetry.

**CoAP (Constrained Application Protocol):** CoAP is a lightweight, RESTful protocol designed for constrained devices and constrained networks such as IoT deployments. It enables communication between devices with limited resources, supporting resource discovery, state transfer, and group communication.

**AMQP (Advanced Message Queuing Protocol):** AMQP is a messaging protocol designed for reliable, asynchronous communication between distributed applications and services. It provides features such as message queuing, routing, and delivery assurance, making it suitable for IoT scenarios with stringent reliability and scalability requirements.

**HTTP/HTTPS (Hypertext Transfer Protocol/Secure):** HTTP/HTTPS are widely used protocols for communication between web clients and servers. They are increasingly used in IoT applications for RESTful APIs, web-based interfaces, and cloud integration, enabling interoperability and data exchange with web services and cloud platforms.

## 2. 5G (Fifth Generation) Networks:

**Low Latency:** 5G networks offer ultra-low latency, with latency as low as a few milliseconds, making them suitable for latency-sensitive edge applications such as autonomous vehicles, augmented reality, and industrial automation.

**High Bandwidth:** 5G provides significantly higher bandwidth compared to previous generations of cellular networks, enabling high-speed data transfer and real-time streaming of high-definition video and multimedia content.

**Massive IoT Connectivity:** 5G supports massive IoT deployments with the ability to connect a large number of devices simultaneously, facilitating IoT use cases such as smart cities, smart grids, and industrial IoT (IIoT) with massive sensor deployments.

**Network Slicing:** 5G enables network slicing, allowing operators to partition the network into multiple virtual networks optimized for specific use cases or industries. Network slicing enables customization, flexibility, and isolation for edge applications with diverse requirements.

## 3. Edge-to-Cloud Connectivity:

**Virtual Private Networks (VPNs):** VPNs establish secure, encrypted tunnels over public networks such as the internet, enabling secure communication between edge devices, gateways, servers, and centralized cloud infrastructure. VPNs ensure data privacy, integrity, and confidentiality in edge-to-cloud communication.

**SD-WAN (Software-Defined Wide Area Network):** SD-WAN technologies optimize wide area network (WAN) connectivity between distributed edge locations, cloud data centers, and centralized cloud infrastructure. SD-WAN solutions provide dynamic routing, traffic optimization, and application-aware policies to improve performance, reliability, and efficiency in edge-to-cloud connectivity.

**Edge-to-Cloud Integration Platforms:** Integration platforms such as Azure IoT Hub, AWS IoT Core, and Google Cloud IoT Core facilitate seamless integration and data exchange between edge devices, gateways, servers, and cloud services. They provide APIs, SDKs, and protocols for edge-to-cloud communication, data ingestion, and analytics in hybrid edge-cloud architectures.

By leveraging these networking technologies, organizations can establish reliable, low-latency communication channels between edge devices, gateways, servers, and centralized cloud infrastructure, enabling efficient data exchange, real-time analytics, and decision-making in edge computing deployments.

Understanding these architectures and technologies is essential for designing, deploying, and managing edge computing solutions that meet the performance, scalability, security, and interoperability requirements of modern applications and services. By leveraging edge infrastructure components, software frameworks, networking technologies, and security measures, organizations can harness the full potential of edge computing to drive innovation and create value in diverse industry verticals.

# 3. EDGE COMPUTING MODELS

## 3.1 Decentralized and Distributed Computing

Decentralized and distributed computing are both paradigms that involve the allocation of computing resources across multiple nodes or devices rather than relying on a single centralized server. While they share similarities, they have distinct characteristics and architectural principles. Here's an overview of decentralized and distributed computing:

## 1. Decentralized Computing:

**Definition:** Decentralized computing refers to a computing paradigm where computational tasks, data storage, and decision-making are distributed across multiple nodes or devices in a network. There is no single point of control or authority, and nodes operate autonomously, making local decisions based on local information.

**Peer-to-Peer (P2P) Networks:** Decentralized computing often relies on peer-to-peer networks, where each node acts as both a client and a server, collaborating with other nodes to perform computational tasks, share resources, and exchange data directly.

**Resilience:** Decentralized computing architectures are inherently resilient to failures and attacks since there is no single point of failure. Even if some nodes fail or are compromised, the network can continue to operate, albeit with reduced capacity or performance.

**Scalability:** Decentralized systems can scale out by adding more nodes to the network, distributing the computational load and improving overall performance. However, the scalability of decentralized systems may be limited by factors such as network bandwidth and communication overhead.

***Examples:*** Blockchain networks, peer-to-peer file sharing systems (e.g., BitTorrent), decentralized social media platforms (e.g., Mastodon), and decentralized autonomous organizations (DAOs) are examples of decentralized computing systems.

## 2. Distributed Computing:

**Definition:** Distributed computing involves the coordinated execution of computational tasks across multiple nodes or devices in a network. Unlike decentralized computing, distributed systems typically have a central coordinator or control mechanism that orchestrates communication and resource allocation among nodes.

**Client-Server Architecture:** Distributed computing often follows a client-server architecture, where clients request services or resources from servers, which handle the processing and provide responses back to clients. However, distributed systems can also involve peer-to-peer communication and collaboration among nodes.

**Resource Sharing:** Distributed systems enable efficient resource sharing and utilization by distributing computational tasks across multiple nodes. This allows for better utilization of hardware resources and improved overall system performance.

**Centralized Control:** Distributed systems may have centralized control mechanisms or distributed coordination algorithms to manage communication, synchronization, and consistency among nodes. These mechanisms ensure that distributed tasks are executed correctly and efficiently.

*Examples:* Cloud computing platforms (e.g., AWS, Azure, Google Cloud), content delivery networks (CDNs), distributed databases (e.g., Cassandra, MongoDB), and distributed computing frameworks (e.g., Apache Hadoop, Apache Spark) are examples of distributed computing systems.

### *Key Differences:*

**Control:** Decentralized computing lacks a central authority or control mechanism, while distributed computing may have centralized control or coordination mechanisms.

**Autonomy:** Nodes in decentralized computing operate autonomously and make local decisions, while nodes in distributed computing may coordinate their actions based on centralized control or consensus algorithms.

**Resilience:** Decentralized systems are inherently resilient to failures, while distributed systems may rely on fault tolerance mechanisms and redundancy to achieve resilience.

**Scalability:** Distributed systems may scale better than decentralized systems due to centralized control and coordination mechanisms, although both paradigms can scale out by adding more nodes.

In summary, decentralized and distributed computing are both important paradigms for distributing computational tasks across multiple nodes or devices. While they share similarities in their goals of achieving fault tolerance, scalability, and resilience, they have distinct characteristics and architectural principles that make them suitable for different types of applications and use cases.

## 3.2 Edge-to-Cloud Continuum

The Edge-to-Cloud continuum refers to the spectrum of computing resources and infrastructure that span from the edge of the network to centralized cloud data centers. This continuum encompasses a range of computing environments and deployment models, each with distinct characteristics and trade-offs. Here's an overview of the Edge-to-Cloud continuum:

## 1. Edge Computing:

**Definition:** Edge computing brings computational resources closer to the source of data generation, enabling real-time or near-real-time processing, analysis, and decision-making at the network edge. Edge computing reduces latency, bandwidth usage, and reliance on centralized cloud infrastructure by processing data locally on edge devices, gateways, or servers.

**Location:** Edge computing resources are deployed at the network edge, which may include edge devices (e.g., sensors, IoT devices), edge gateways, and edge servers located in close proximity to where data is generated. Edge computing resources may be deployed at the network edge, enterprise premises, or industrial facilities.

**Use Cases:** Edge computing is well-suited for latency-sensitive applications, real-time analytics, and data processing in distributed IoT, industrial automation, smart cities, and telecommunications. Examples include autonomous vehicles, smart grids, remote monitoring, and predictive maintenance.

## 2. Fog Computing:

**Definition:** Fog computing extends cloud computing capabilities to the edge of the network, bringing computational resources closer to edge devices and endpoints. Fog computing introduces a hierarchical architecture with multiple layers of fog nodes, ranging from the edge to the cloud, to support distributed data processing and analytics.

**Hierarchy:** Fog computing introduces intermediate fog nodes or gateways between edge devices and centralized cloud infrastructure, enabling data aggregation, preprocessing, and filtering closer to the source of data generation. Fog nodes may perform edge analytics, caching, or storage to optimize data flow and reduce latency.

Scalability: Fog computing supports scalable and flexible deployment models, allowing organizations to distribute computational tasks across multiple layers of the network hierarchy. Fog nodes can dynamically allocate resources based on workload requirements and optimize resource usage in distributed edge deployments.

### 3. Cloud Computing:

**Definition:** Cloud computing centralizes computational resources, storage, and services in centralized data centers managed by cloud service providers. Cloud computing offers on-demand access to virtualized resources, scalability, and flexibility for deploying and managing applications and services over the internet.

**Location:** Cloud computing resources are hosted in centralized data centers operated by cloud service providers such as Amazon Web Services (AWS), Microsoft Azure, and Google Cloud Platform (GCP). Cloud data centers may be located in multiple regions or availability zones to ensure redundancy, fault tolerance, and high availability.

**Use Cases:** Cloud computing supports a wide range of applications and workloads, including web hosting, software as a service (SaaS), platform as a service (PaaS), and infrastructure as a service (IaaS). Cloud services provide scalability, reliability, and security for deploying mission-critical applications, big data analytics, and machine learning workloads.

**4. Hybrid and Multi-Cloud Deployments:**

**Definition:** Hybrid and multi-cloud deployments combine edge, fog, and cloud computing resources to create a distributed computing infrastructure that spans across multiple environments and platforms. These deployment models leverage the strengths of edge, fog, and cloud computing to optimize performance, scalability, and cost-effectiveness for diverse workloads and use cases.

**Integration:** Hybrid and multi-cloud deployments require seamless integration and interoperability between edge, fog, and cloud environments. Integration platforms, APIs, and protocols facilitate data exchange, workload migration, and orchestration across distributed computing resources.

**Flexibility:** Hybrid and multi-cloud deployments offer flexibility and agility for organizations to leverage edge, fog, and cloud computing resources based on workload requirements, cost considerations, and performance objectives. They provide a scalable and adaptable infrastructure for deploying distributed applications and services in dynamic environments.

In summary, the Edge-to-Cloud continuum encompasses a range of computing environments and deployment models, including edge computing, fog computing, cloud computing, and hybrid/multi-cloud deployments. Organizations can leverage the Edge-to-Cloud continuum to design and deploy distributed computing solutions that meet their specific requirements for performance, scalability, reliability, and cost-effectiveness in diverse applications and use cases.

## 3.3 Hierarchical Edge Architectures

Hierarchical edge architectures are structured frameworks that organize edge computing resources into distinct layers or tiers, each serving specific functions and roles within the overall architecture. This hierarchical approach facilitates efficient resource management, workload distribution, and data processing in edge computing deployments. Here's an in-depth look at hierarchical edge architectures:

## 1. Edge Devices:

**Definition:** Edge devices are the endpoints where data is generated or consumed, such as sensors, actuators, IoT devices, and edge clients like smartphones or tablets. These devices are situated at the network's edge, closest to the data source.

**Functions:** Edge devices capture real-time data from sensors, monitor local conditions, and initiate actions based on predefined rules or algorithms. They serve as the entry point for data into the edge architecture and often perform initial data preprocessing tasks.

*Examples:* Industrial sensors in manufacturing plants, smart cameras in surveillance systems, and wearable health monitors are common examples of edge devices.

## 2. Edge Gateways:

**Definition:** Edge gateways serve as intermediaries between edge devices and higher-level layers in the architecture, such as edge servers or cloud infrastructure. These gateways aggregate, filter, and preprocess data from multiple edge devices before transmitting it to higher layers.

**Functions:** Edge gateways perform data aggregation, protocol translation, and data normalization tasks. They also handle communication with edge devices using various protocols, ensuring compatibility and interoperability within the edge architecture.

*Examples:* Industrial IoT gateways, smart home hubs, and edge routers are typical examples of edge gateways.

## 3. Edge Servers:

**Definition:** Edge servers are computing nodes located closer to the edge devices than centralized cloud servers. These servers provide computational resources for processing, analyzing, and storing data locally.

**Functions:** Edge servers execute edge applications, perform real-time analytics, and store frequently accessed data locally. They facilitate low-latency data processing and decision-making at the edge, reducing reliance on centralized cloud resources.

*Examples:* Edge computing nodes, micro data centers, and cloudlets are common examples of edge servers deployed in hierarchical edge architectures.

## 4. Cloud Infrastructure:

**Definition:** Cloud infrastructure consists of centralized data centers managed by cloud service providers. These data centers offer scalable computing resources, storage, and services accessible over the internet.

**Functions:** Cloud infrastructure complements edge computing by providing additional computational capacity, storage, and services for tasks that cannot be efficiently performed at the edge. It supports long-term data storage, complex analytics, and resource-intensive workloads.

***Examples:*** Public cloud platforms like AWS, Azure, and Google Cloud provide cloud infrastructure services for deploying, managing, and scaling applications across distributed edge environments.

Hierarchical edge architectures provide a structured framework for deploying and managing edge computing solutions effectively. By organizing edge resources into distinct layers, these architectures optimize resource utilization, streamline data processing, and facilitate seamless integration between edge and cloud environments. They enable organizations to harness the benefits of edge computing while leveraging the scalability and flexibility of centralized cloud infrastructure.

## 3.4 Mobile Edge Computing (MEC)

Mobile Edge Computing (MEC) is a distributed computing paradigm that extends cloud computing capabilities to the edge of cellular networks, closer to mobile users and devices. MEC aims to deliver low-latency, high-bandwidth, and context-aware services by deploying computational resources, storage, and networking functions at the edge of the network infrastructure. Here's an overview of Mobile Edge Computing:

## 1. Definition and Concept:

**Definition:** Mobile Edge Computing (MEC), also known as Multi-Access Edge Computing, is a network architecture that brings cloud computing resources closer to mobile users and devices at the edge of cellular networks. It enables applications and services to run on edge servers located within the Radio Access Network (RAN) or in close proximity to base stations.

**Concept:** MEC leverages the proximity of edge servers to mobile users and devices to reduce latency, improve network efficiency, and enable new types of applications and services. By processing data closer to the source, MEC enhances the user experience for mobile applications, supports real-time analytics, and enables new use cases such as augmented reality, virtual reality, and Internet of Things (IoT) applications.

## 2. Architecture and Components:

**Edge Servers:** MEC architecture includes edge servers deployed at the edge of cellular networks, typically within base stations or aggregation points. These edge servers host virtualized infrastructure, application containers, and network functions to support edge computing services.

**Radio Access Network (RAN):** MEC integrates with the RAN infrastructure to enable seamless interaction between edge servers and mobile devices. It may involve standardizing interfaces and protocols for communication between edge servers and base stations.

**MEC Platform:** MEC platforms provide tools, APIs, and development frameworks for deploying, managing, and orchestrating edge applications and services. They abstract the underlying infrastructure and provide a unified interface for developers to build and deploy MEC applications.

### 3. Key Features and Benefits:

**Low Latency:** By processing data closer to the source, MEC reduces latency for mobile applications and services, enabling real-time interactions and responsiveness.

High Bandwidth: MEC leverages high-speed, low-latency connections within the cellular network infrastructure to deliver high-bandwidth services such as video streaming, gaming, and augmented reality.

**Context Awareness:** MEC applications can leverage contextual information such as location, network conditions, and user preferences to personalize services and optimize resource allocation.

## 4. Use Cases and Applications:

**Enhanced Mobile Broadband (eMBB):** MEC enables high-definition video streaming, immersive gaming, and other bandwidth-intensive applications on mobile devices.

**Ultra-Reliable Low-Latency Communications (URLLC):** MEC supports mission-critical applications that require ultra-low latency and high reliability, such as autonomous vehicles, industrial automation, and remote surgery.

**Massive Machine Type Communications (mMTC):** MEC facilitates the deployment of IoT applications and services by providing edge computing capabilities for processing IoT data and managing IoT devices.

## 5. Standards and Ecosystem:

**ETSI MEC:** The European Telecommunications Standards Institute (ETSI) defines specifications and standards for Mobile Edge Computing, including architecture, interfaces, and APIs.

**Industry Collaboration:** Various industry groups and consortia, including the GSMA and Open Edge Computing, collaborate to develop interoperable solutions and promote adoption of MEC technology.

Mobile Edge Computing (MEC) is poised to transform mobile networks by bringing cloud computing capabilities closer to mobile users and devices. By reducing latency, improving network efficiency, and enabling new use cases, MEC enhances the mobile user experience and unlocks new opportunities for innovation in mobile applications and services.

## 3.5 Industrial Internet of Things (IIoT) Edge Computing

Industrial Internet of Things (IIoT) Edge Computing refers to the convergence of Industrial Internet of Things (IIoT) and edge computing technologies within industrial environments. It involves the deployment of edge computing infrastructure and intelligence at the network edge, closer to industrial devices, sensors, and machinery, to enable real-time data processing, analysis, and control. Here's a detailed overview:

## *1. Definition and Concept:*

**Definition:** IIoT Edge Computing combines the capabilities of IIoT, which involves connecting industrial equipment and systems to the internet to gather data and enable remote monitoring and control, with edge computing, which brings computational resources closer to the data source to reduce latency and enable faster decision-making.

**Concept:** IIoT Edge Computing aims to enhance industrial operations by processing and analyzing data locally at the edge of the network, near where it is generated. This allows for real-time insights, predictive analytics, and automated decision-making without the need to send data to centralized cloud servers, reducing latency and bandwidth requirements.

## *2. Architecture and Components:*

**Edge Devices and Sensors:** IIoT Edge Computing relies on a variety of industrial sensors, actuators, and devices deployed throughout the industrial environment to collect data on parameters such as temperature, pressure, vibration, and machine status.

**Edge Gateways:** Edge gateways are deployed at the edge of the network to aggregate, preprocess, and filter data from edge devices before transmitting it to higher-level systems or cloud platforms. They may also perform data normalization and protocol translation tasks.

**Edge Servers:** Edge servers, located within the industrial premises or at the edge of the network, host edge computing applications, analytics algorithms, and control logic. They provide computational resources for processing data locally and executing real-time control actions.

### 3. Key Features and Benefits:

**Real-Time Data Processing:** IIoT Edge Computing enables real-time processing and analysis of industrial data at the network edge, allowing for immediate insights and actionable intelligence to optimize industrial processes and operations.

**Predictive Maintenance:** By analyzing sensor data locally, IIoT Edge Computing can detect equipment anomalies and predict failures before they occur, enabling proactive maintenance to minimize downtime and reduce maintenance costs.

**Improved Efficiency:** Edge computing allows for more efficient use of network bandwidth and reduces the need to transmit large volumes of data to centralized cloud servers for processing, leading to improved network efficiency and reduced operational costs.

### 4. Use Cases and Applications:

**Condition Monitoring:** IIoT Edge Computing enables real-time monitoring of equipment health and performance, detecting abnormalities and deviations from normal operating conditions to prevent unplanned downtime and optimize maintenance schedules.

**Predictive Maintenance:** By analyzing sensor data at the edge, IIoT Edge Computing can predict equipment failures before they occur, allowing maintenance teams to take preventive actions and avoid costly breakdowns.

**Process Optimization:** Edge computing facilitates real-time analysis of production data to identify inefficiencies, optimize production processes, and improve overall operational efficiency.

**Quality Control:** IIoT Edge Computing can be used to monitor and control quality parameters during manufacturing processes, ensuring that products meet quality standards and specifications.

## 5. Challenges and Considerations:

**Interoperability:** Integrating heterogeneous industrial systems and legacy equipment with IIoT Edge Computing solutions may require standardized protocols, interfaces, and integration frameworks to ensure interoperability and seamless data exchange.

**Security:** IIoT Edge Computing introduces new security challenges, including data privacy, integrity, and protection against cyber threats. Robust security measures such as encryption, authentication, and access control are essential to safeguard industrial systems and data.

**Scalability:** IIoT Edge Computing solutions must be scalable to accommodate growing numbers of edge devices, sensors, and data sources while maintaining performance, reliability, and manageability.

## 6. Industry Standards and Initiatives:

**OPC UA:** The OPC Unified Architecture (UA) standardizes communication and data exchange between industrial devices, systems, and applications, facilitating interoperability and integration in IIoT Edge Computing deployments.

**ISA-95:** The ISA-95 standard defines models and terminology for integrating enterprise and control systems in industrial automation and manufacturing environments, providing guidelines for IIoT Edge Computing architectures.

In summary, Industrial Internet of Things (IIoT) Edge Computing offers significant potential to enhance industrial operations by enabling real-time data processing, predictive analytics, and automated control at the network edge. By deploying edge computing infrastructure within industrial environments, organizations can achieve greater operational efficiency, reduced downtime, and improved product quality, leading to increased competitiveness and profitability.

# 4. EDGE COMPUTING APPLICATIONS

Edge computing has a wide range of applications across various industries, enabling real-time processing, low-latency responses, and data analysis closer to the data source. Here are some common applications of edge computing.

## 4.1 Real-time Data Analytics

Real-time data analytics involves the collection, processing, and analysis of data as it is generated, allowing organizations to make informed decisions and take immediate action based on up-to-date information. Here's how it works:

Fig 1. Data Analytics

## 1. Data Collection:

- Real-time data analytics begins with the collection of data from various sources, such as sensors, IoT devices, social media feeds, website interactions, and transactional systems.
- Data is ingested continuously into a data processing system, where it is stored, processed, and analyzed in real-time.

## 2. Stream Processing:

- Stream processing engines are used to process data as it flows through the system, enabling real-time analysis and insights.
- Data streams are processed in small, incremental batches or micro-batches, allowing for low-latency processing and quick response times.

## 3. Data Analysis:

- Real-time analytics algorithms are applied to streaming data to identify patterns, trends, anomalies, and other actionable insights.
- Techniques such as machine learning, predictive analytics, and complex event processing are used to

extract meaningful information from the data in real-time.

## 4. Visualization and Dashboards:

- Real-time analytics platforms often include visualization tools and dashboards that allow users to monitor key metrics, KPIs, and performance indicators in real-time.

- Interactive dashboards provide users with the ability to drill down into the data, explore trends, and uncover insights dynamically.

## 5. Decision Making and Action:

- Real-time insights empower organizations to make timely decisions and take immediate action based on changing conditions and emerging opportunities or threats.

- Automated alerts, notifications, and triggers can be configured to notify stakeholders of critical events or deviations from expected outcomes in real-time.

***Benefits:***

*Faster Decision Making:* Real-time data analytics enables organizations to respond quickly to changing conditions, market dynamics, and customer needs.

*Improved Operational Efficiency:* By monitoring and analyzing data in real-time, organizations can identify inefficiencies, optimize processes, and reduce downtime.

*Enhanced Customer Experience:* Real-time insights enable personalized interactions, targeted marketing campaigns, and proactive customer service, improving satisfaction and loyalty.

*Competitive Advantage:* Organizations that leverage real-time data analytics gain a competitive edge by staying ahead of the curve, identifying opportunities, and mitigating risks in real-time.

***Challenges:***

*Data Quality and Consistency:* Ensuring the accuracy, completeness, and consistency of real-time data can be challenging, especially when dealing with high-volume, high-velocity data streams.

*Scalability:* Scaling real-time analytics systems to handle increasing data volumes and user concurrency requires robust infrastructure and resource management.

*Integration Complexity:* Integrating real-time analytics with existing systems, applications, and workflows can be complex and require careful planning and execution.

*Privacy and Security:* Real-time data analytics raise concerns about data privacy, security, and compliance, particularly when dealing with sensitive or regulated data.

Overall, real-time data analytics empowers organizations to gain valuable insights, drive innovation, and achieve strategic objectives in today's fast-paced, data-driven business environment.

## 4.2 Internet of Things (IoT) and Sensor Networks

The Internet of Things (IoT) and sensor networks are revolutionizing how we interact with technology and the world around us. Here's a breakdown:

### *Internet of Things (IoT):*

The IoT refers to the network of physical devices, vehicles, home appliances, and other items embedded with electronics, software, sensors, actuators, and connectivity which enables these objects to connect and exchange data. The idea is to create a smart environment where everything is interconnected, making processes more efficient, improving decision-making, and enhancing overall quality of life.

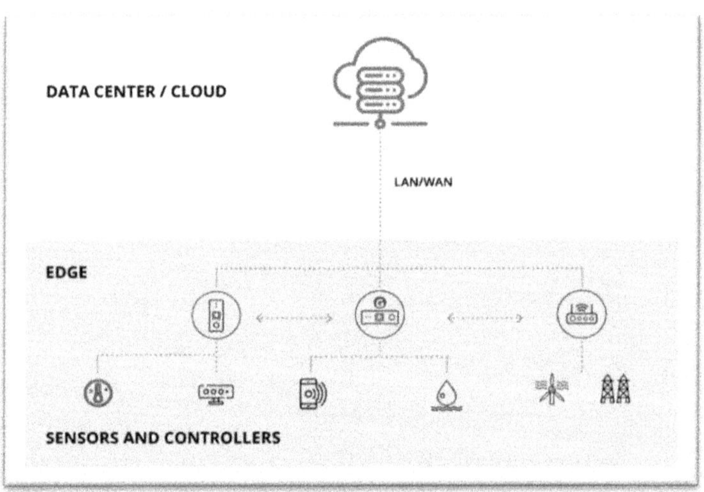


Fig 2. IoT Sensors

### *Sensor Networks:*

Sensor networks are a key component of the IoT ecosystem. These networks consist of spatially distributed autonomous sensors to monitor physical or environmental conditions, such as temperature, humidity, pressure, motion, sound, and so on. These sensors collect data and transmit it to a central hub or server for processing and analysis.

***Applications:***

*Smart Home:* IoT-enabled devices like smart thermostats, lights, and security systems allow homeowners to control and monitor their home remotely.

*Healthcare:* Wearable devices equipped with sensors can monitor vital signs, track physical activity, and provide valuable health insights to users and healthcare providers.

*Industrial IoT (IIoT):* In manufacturing and industrial settings, IoT sensors can monitor equipment performance, predict maintenance needs, and optimize production processes.

*Smart Cities:* Sensor networks deployed throughout cities can monitor traffic flow, air quality, waste management, and other aspects of urban life to improve efficiency and sustainability.

*Agriculture:* IoT devices and sensor networks help farmers monitor soil moisture, temperature, and crop health, enabling precision agriculture and better resource management.

### Challenges:

*Security:* With the massive amount of data being collected and transmitted, ensuring the security and privacy of IoT devices and networks is paramount.

*Interoperability:* Devices from different manufacturers may use different protocols and standards, making it challenging to ensure seamless communication and integration.

*Scalability:* As the number of connected devices continues to grow exponentially, scaling IoT systems to accommodate this growth becomes increasingly complex.

*Power Consumption:* Many IoT devices are battery-powered, so optimizing power consumption to prolong battery life is crucial, especially for devices in remote or inaccessible locations.

Overall, the IoT and sensor networks have the potential to transform industries, improve efficiency, and enhance our quality of life, but addressing the associated challenges is essential for realizing this potential.

## 4.3 Smart Cities and Infrastructure Management

Smart cities leverage advanced technology and data-driven approaches to enhance the efficiency, sustainability, and livability of urban environments. Here's how smart cities and infrastructure management intersect:

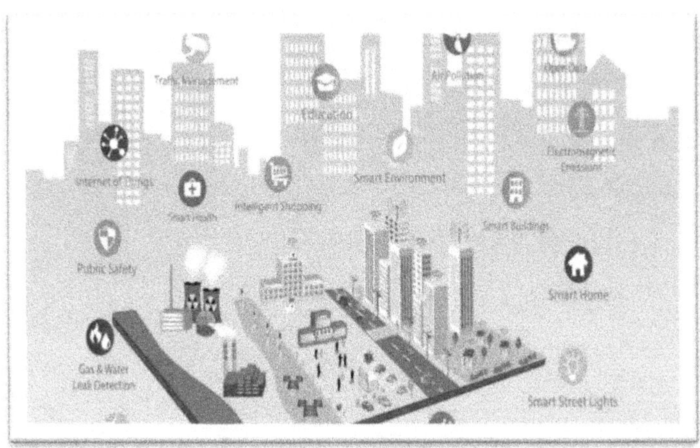


Fig 3. Smart City

## *1. Infrastructure Monitoring and Maintenance:*

*Sensor Networks:* Smart cities deploy sensor networks to monitor the condition of critical infrastructure such as bridges, roads, water pipes, and electrical grids. These sensors detect anomalies, deterioration, or failures in real-time, enabling proactive maintenance and minimizing downtime.

*Predictive Analytics:* Data collected from sensors and other sources enable predictive analytics, allowing city officials to anticipate maintenance needs and prioritize repairs to prevent costly infrastructure failures.

## 2. Transportation Management:

*Traffic Flow Optimization:* Smart cities use IoT-enabled traffic sensors, cameras, and algorithms to monitor traffic flow in real-time. This data helps optimize traffic signal timing, reroute vehicles during congestion, and improve overall transportation efficiency.

*Public Transit Systems:* Integrated smart transit systems provide real-time information to commuters about bus and train schedules, delays, and alternative routes, encouraging the use of public transportation and reducing congestion.

## 3. Energy Efficiency and Sustainability:

*Smart Grids:* IoT devices and sensors in electrical grids enable utilities to monitor energy consumption, detect outages, and manage demand more efficiently. Smart grids also facilitate the integration of renewable energy sources and support energy conservation initiatives.

*Building Management Systems:* Smart buildings equipped with IoT sensors and automation systems optimize energy usage by adjusting lighting, heating, and cooling based on occupancy patterns and environmental conditions.

### 4. Waste Management:

*Bin Monitoring:* Smart waste bins equipped with sensors can detect when they're full and automatically schedule pickups, optimizing waste collection routes and reducing unnecessary trips.

*Recycling Initiatives:* Smart cities use data analytics to track recycling rates, identify areas for improvement, and implement targeted education and incentive programs to promote recycling and reduce landfill waste.

### 5. Citizen Engagement and Quality of Life:

*Digital Platforms:* Smart cities provide online platforms and mobile apps for citizens to report issues such as potholes, graffiti, or streetlight outages. These platforms streamline communication between residents and city officials, leading to faster response times and improved service delivery.

*Community Services:* IoT-enabled amenities such as smart streetlights, public Wi-Fi hotspots, and interactive kiosks enhance public safety, accessibility, and connectivity, contributing to a higher quality of life for residents.

### Challenges:

*Data Security and Privacy:* As smart cities collect and analyze vast amounts of data, ensuring the security and privacy of this information is critical to maintaining public trust.

*Interoperability:* Integrating diverse systems and technologies from multiple vendors can be challenging, requiring open standards and interoperable platforms.

*Digital Divide:* Ensuring equitable access to smart city technologies and digital services is essential to prevent exacerbating socioeconomic disparities.

By leveraging technology and data-driven solutions, smart cities can address these challenges and improve the efficiency, sustainability, and resilience of urban infrastructure for the benefit of all citizens.

## 4.4 Autonomous Vehicles and Transportation

Autonomous vehicles (AVs) are revolutionizing transportation by leveraging advanced technologies to operate without human intervention. Here's how AVs are impacting the transportation industry:

Fig 4. Autonomous Vehicles and Transportation

## 1. Increased Safety:

- AVs are equipped with sensors, cameras, radar, lidar, and AI algorithms that enable them to perceive their surroundings and navigate safely.

- By eliminating human error, which is a leading cause of accidents, AVs have the potential to significantly reduce traffic collisions and fatalities.

## 2. Improved Efficiency:

- AVs can optimize routes, speeds, and driving behaviors to reduce congestion and improve traffic flow.
- They can communicate with each other and with infrastructure, enabling coordinated movements and smoother traffic patterns.

## 3. Enhanced Accessibility:

- AVs have the potential to increase mobility options for individuals who are unable to drive due to age, disability, or other reasons.
- They can provide on-demand transportation services, making it easier for people to access jobs, healthcare, education, and recreational activities.

## 4. Environmental Benefits:

- AVs can improve fuel efficiency and reduce emissions through more efficient driving behaviors and the adoption of electric and alternative fuel technologies.

+ By reducing congestion and optimizing traffic flow, AVs can also contribute to lower greenhouse gas emissions and improved air quality in urban areas.

## 5. Transformative Urban Planning:

+ The widespread adoption of AVs is likely to impact urban design, land use patterns, and transportation infrastructure.

+ Cities may need to rethink roadways, parking, and public transit systems to accommodate AVs effectively and create more livable, sustainable communities.

## Challenges:

*Technology Development:* Achieving full autonomy in all driving conditions remains a significant technical challenge, particularly in complex urban environments and adverse weather conditions.

*Regulatory Framework:* Developing comprehensive regulations and standards for AVs is essential to ensure safety, liability, and interoperability with existing transportation systems.

*Public Acceptance:* Building public trust and acceptance of AVs will require education, demonstration of safety benefits, and addressing concerns about job displacement and privacy.

*Cybersecurity:* Securing AVs against cyber threats and attacks is critical to prevent unauthorized access, tampering, or malicious interference with vehicle systems.

As technology continues to advance and regulatory frameworks evolve, autonomous vehicles have the potential to transform transportation, offering safer, more efficient, and accessible mobility solutions for communities around the world.

## 4.5 Healthcare and Telemedicine

Healthcare and telemedicine are intersecting to revolutionize the delivery of medical services, especially in the context of remote patient care. Here's how:

Fig 5. Healthcare and Telemedicine

## 1. Remote Consultations:

- Telemedicine enables healthcare providers to conduct remote consultations with patients using video conferencing, phone calls, or secure messaging platforms.
- Patients can receive medical advice, diagnosis, and treatment recommendations from the comfort of their homes, eliminating the need for in-person visits, especially for routine check-ups and follow-ups.

## 2. Access to Specialists:

- Telemedicine allows patients to access specialists and healthcare services that may not be available locally. This is particularly beneficial for individuals living in rural or underserved areas with limited access to specialty care.

## 3. Monitoring and Management:

- Remote patient monitoring technologies enable healthcare providers to track patients' vital signs, symptoms, and medication adherence remotely.
- Patients with chronic conditions can receive ongoing monitoring and management, allowing for early intervention and proactive healthcare.

## 4. Telemedicine Platforms:

- Dedicated telemedicine platforms and mobile health apps connect patients with healthcare providers, facilitating appointment scheduling, medical record access, and secure communication.
- These platforms often integrate with electronic health record (EHR) systems, ensuring continuity of care and seamless information exchange between providers.

## 5. Emergency Care and Triage:

- Telemedicine is increasingly being used for emergency medical consultations and triage,

allowing healthcare providers to assess patients remotely and determine the appropriate level of care.
+ Telemedicine can help reduce unnecessary emergency room visits and hospital admissions by providing timely medical advice and directing patients to the most appropriate care setting.

## 6. Education and Training:

+ Telemedicine platforms are used for medical education, training, and continuing medical education (CME) programs.
+ Healthcare professionals can participate in virtual conferences, webinars, and online courses to stay updated on the latest medical research, treatments, and technologies.

### *Challenges:*

*Regulatory and Reimbursement Policies:* Telemedicine regulations and reimbursement policies vary by region and can impact the adoption and scalability of telemedicine services.

*Technological Infrastructure:* Access to reliable internet connectivity and technology devices is essential for both patients and healthcare providers to participate in telemedicine consultations.

*Privacy and Security:* Protecting patient privacy and securing sensitive health information transmitted during telemedicine consultations is critical to maintaining trust and compliance with healthcare regulations.

As telemedicine continues to evolve and become more integrated into healthcare delivery models, it has the potential to improve access to care, enhance patient outcomes, and reduce healthcare costs by providing more efficient and convenient healthcare services.

## 4.6 Retail and Customer Experience Enhancement

Retailers are increasingly leveraging technology to enhance the customer experience and drive sales. Here's how technology is transforming the retail industry:

### 1. Personalized Shopping Experience:

- Retailers use data analytics and customer relationship management (CRM) systems to gather insights about customer preferences, purchase history, and behavior.

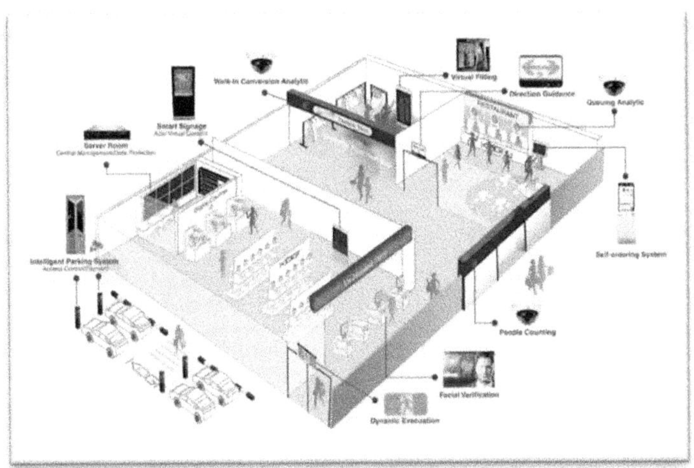

Fig 6. Retail and Customer Experience Enhancement

+ Personalized recommendations, targeted promotions, and customized product offerings are delivered to customers through online platforms, mobile apps, and in-store experiences.

## 2. Omnichannel Retailing:

+ Retailers offer a seamless shopping experience across multiple channels, including brick-and-mortar stores, e-commerce websites, mobile apps, social media platforms, and virtual marketplaces.

+ Customers can browse products, make purchases, and interact with brands through their preferred channels, with options for in-store pickup, home delivery, or shipping to alternate locations.

## 3. Augmented Reality (AR) and Virtual Reality (VR):

- AR and VR technologies enable retailers to create immersive shopping experiences that allow customers to visualize products in real-world environments.

- Virtual try-on solutions for apparel, cosmetics, and accessories, as well as virtual showrooms for furniture and home decor, enhance the online shopping experience and reduce the need for returns.

## 4. Contactless Payments and Self-Service Kiosks:

- Contactless payment options, such as mobile wallets and tap-to-pay systems, provide convenience and security for customers during checkout.

- Self-service kiosks and automated checkout systems allow customers to scan, pay, and bag their purchases independently, reducing wait times and enhancing efficiency in-store.

## 5. Inventory Management and Fulfillment:

- Retailers utilize inventory management software and supply chain analytics to optimize inventory levels, reduce stockouts, and improve order fulfillment processes.
- Advanced logistics and fulfillment solutions, including same-day delivery, curbside pickup, and click-and-collect services, offer convenience and flexibility for customers.

## 6. Enhanced In-Store Experiences:

- Retailers incorporate interactive displays, digital signage, and smart mirrors into their store layouts to engage customers and showcase products.
- In-store events, workshops, and demonstrations provide opportunities for experiential marketing and community engagement, fostering brand loyalty and customer satisfaction.

*Challenges:*

*Data Privacy and Security:* Collecting and managing customer data raises concerns about privacy and security. Retailers must implement robust cybersecurity measures and comply with data protection regulations.

*Technology Integration:* Integrating disparate technology systems and platforms can be complex and require investments in infrastructure, training, and organizational change management.

*Digital Divide:* Ensuring equitable access to technology for all customers, including those with limited digital literacy or internet connectivity, is essential to prevent exclusion and promote inclusivity in retail experiences.

By embracing technology and innovation, retailers can create more engaging, personalized, and convenient shopping experiences that drive customer satisfaction, loyalty, and long-term business success.

# 5. SECURITY, PRIVACY AND ETHICAL CONSIDERATIONS

## 5.1 Security Challenges and Threats

Security challenges and threats are significant concerns in the realm of edge computing, primarily due to the distributed nature of the infrastructure and the diverse range of connected devices. Here are some key security challenges and threats associated with edge computing:

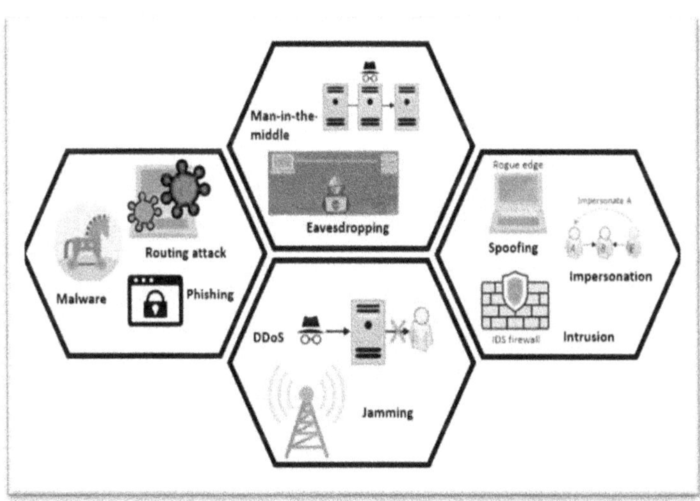


Fig 1. Security and Privacy Attacks

## 1. Data Privacy and Compliance:

- Edge devices often collect and process sensitive data, raising concerns about data privacy and compliance with regulations such as GDPR, HIPAA, and CCPA.
- Ensuring that data is encrypted, securely transmitted, and properly handled at the edge is essential to protect user privacy and comply with regulatory requirements.

## 2. Endpoint Security:

- Edge devices, including IoT sensors, gateways, and edge servers, are vulnerable to security breaches and cyberattacks.
- Weaknesses in device firmware, operating systems, and communication protocols can be exploited by attackers to gain unauthorized access, steal data, or launch denial-of-service attacks.

## 3. Network Security:

- Edge networks are susceptible to network-based attacks, such as man-in-the-middle attacks, packet sniffing, and spoofing.

- Insecure network configurations, lack of encryption, and inadequate access controls can expose edge devices and data to interception and manipulation by malicious actors.

## 4. Insider Threats:

- Insider threats, including malicious insiders and compromised devices, pose a significant risk to edge computing environments.

- Employees or contractors with access to edge devices and systems may abuse their privileges or inadvertently introduce vulnerabilities, leading to data breaches or service disruptions.

## 5. Supply Chain Risks:

- Supply chain attacks targeting hardware and software components pose a growing threat to edge computing infrastructure.

- Malicious actors may tamper with hardware components, inject malware into firmware or software updates, or compromise third-party vendors to gain access to edge devices and networks.

## 6. Edge-to-Cloud Security:

- Securing the communication between edge devices and centralized cloud services is critical to prevent data interception, tampering, and unauthorized access.

- Secure protocols, such as TLS/SSL, VPNs, and encryption technologies, are used to establish secure connections and protect data in transit.

## 7. Scalability and Management:

- Managing security at scale in distributed edge environments can be challenging due to the large number of devices and diverse locations.

- Deploying security updates, patches, and configuration changes to edge devices in a timely manner requires robust management tools and processes.

## 8. Physical Security:

- Physical security measures are essential to protect edge computing infrastructure from theft, vandalism, and tampering.

➕ Securing edge facilities, access points, and equipment against physical threats helps safeguard sensitive data and ensure the integrity of edge operations.

Addressing these security challenges requires a holistic approach that combines technological solutions, risk management strategies, and industry best practices. Organizations must prioritize security throughout the entire lifecycle of edge computing deployments, from design and implementation to ongoing monitoring and incident response. Collaborative efforts among stakeholders, including vendors, developers, regulators, and end-users, are essential to mitigate security risks and build trust in edge computing technologies.

## 5.2 Data Privacy and Compliance

Data privacy and compliance are critical considerations in any data-driven environment, including edge computing. Here's how organizations address data privacy and compliance challenges in the context of edge computing:

## 1. Data Minimization:

- Adopting a data minimization approach involves collecting and storing only the data that is necessary for the intended purpose.

- By minimizing data collection at the edge, organizations reduce the risk of privacy breaches and ensure compliance with data protection regulations.

## 2. Encryption and Anonymization:

- Encrypting data both in transit and at rest helps protect sensitive information from unauthorized access or interception.

- Anonymizing or pseudonymizing personal data before storage or transmission further reduces the risk of privacy violations.

## 3. Consent Management:

- Implementing robust consent management processes ensures that individuals are informed about the collection, processing, and use of their data.
- Organizations should obtain explicit consent from data subjects before collecting or processing their

personal information, especially in cases where consent is required by law.

## 4. Secure Data Transmission:

- Utilizing secure communication protocols, such as TLS/SSL and VPNs, helps safeguard data as it travels between edge devices, gateways, and centralized systems.

- Implementing encryption and authentication mechanisms ensures the confidentiality, integrity, and authenticity of data in transit.

## 5. Data Localization:

- Some jurisdictions have regulations that require certain types of data to be stored and processed within the geographical boundaries of the country or region.

- Adhering to data localization requirements ensures compliance with local laws and regulations governing the handling of sensitive data.

## 6. Privacy by Design and Default:

- Incorporating privacy principles into the design and development of edge computing systems ensures that privacy considerations are addressed from the outset.

- Privacy-enhancing technologies, such as differential privacy and homomorphic encryption, can be integrated into edge computing solutions to protect privacy by default.

## 7. Data Life cycle Management:

- Implementing data lifecycle management policies helps organizations manage data in a compliant manner throughout its lifecycle, from collection and processing to storage and disposal.

- Organizations should establish procedures for data retention, archival, and deletion to minimize the risk of unauthorized access or data breaches.

## 8. Regulatory Compliance:

- Staying informed about relevant data protection regulations, such as GDPR, CCPA, and HIPAA, is essential for ensuring compliance with legal requirements.

* Organizations should conduct regular assessments to ensure that their edge computing deployments comply with applicable laws and regulations governing data privacy and security.

## 9. Third-Party Risk Management:

* Assessing the security and privacy practices of third-party vendors and service providers is critical for managing risks associated with outsourcing edge computing services.

* Organizations should establish contractual agreements and security protocols to hold third parties accountable for protecting data and complying with privacy requirements.

By implementing these measures and adopting a privacy-centric approach to edge computing, organizations can enhance data protection, build trust with customers, and mitigate the risk of privacy breaches and regulatory penalties.

### 5.3 Edge vs. Cloud Security

Edge and cloud security are both essential components of a comprehensive cybersecurity strategy, but they address different aspects of security due to the distinct characteristics of edge and cloud computing environments. Here's a comparison of edge vs. cloud security:

**Edge Security:**

***Distributed Nature:***

- Edge computing involves decentralized infrastructure, with computing resources located closer to the data source.

- Edge devices, such as sensors, gateways, and edge servers, are often deployed in remote or uncontrolled environments, increasing the risk of physical tampering, theft, or unauthorized access.

***Limited Resources:***

- Edge devices typically have limited processing power, memory, and storage capacity compared to centralized cloud servers.

- Security measures implemented at the edge must be resource-efficient and lightweight to minimize performance impact and operational overhead.

### *Local Threats:*

- Edge computing environments are susceptible to local threats, such as malware infections, insider attacks, and physical tampering.

- Protecting edge devices against these threats requires robust endpoint security solutions, including antivirus software, intrusion detection systems, and device authentication mechanisms.

### *Network Connectivity:*

- Edge devices communicate with each other and with centralized systems over local networks, cellular networks, or the internet.
- Securing network communications at the edge involves implementing encryption, access controls, and intrusion prevention measures to protect data in transit.

### *Edge-to-Cloud Integration:*

- Integrating edge devices with cloud services requires secure communication channels and authentication mechanisms to establish trust between edge nodes and cloud servers.

- Edge-to-cloud security protocols, such as TLS/SSL, VPNs, and mutual authentication, help ensure the confidentiality, integrity, and authenticity of data exchanged between edge and cloud environments.

### Cloud Security:

### *Centralized Infrastructure:*

- Cloud computing involves centralized data centers operated by cloud service providers, which host and manage computing resources on behalf of customers.

- Cloud providers implement robust physical security measures, access controls, and compliance certifications to protect data and infrastructure within their facilities.

### *Scalability and Flexibility:*

- Cloud environments offer scalable and flexible infrastructure services, enabling organizations to deploy and manage applications and workloads across geographically distributed data centers.

- Cloud security solutions, such as firewalls, intrusion detection systems, and identity and access management (IAM) tools, help organizations secure their cloud resources and data.

### *Shared Responsibility Model:*

- Cloud providers operate under a shared responsibility model, where they are responsible for the security of the cloud infrastructure, while customers are responsible for securing their data and applications deployed in the cloud.

- Customers must implement appropriate security controls, encryption, and access management policies to protect their assets in the cloud.

***Compliance and Auditing:***

- Cloud providers offer compliance certifications, audit trails, and logging capabilities to help customers meet regulatory requirements and industry standards.

- Organizations can leverage cloud security services, such as security information and event management (SIEM) platforms and cloud security posture management (CSPM) tools, to monitor and manage security risks in the cloud.

In summary, while both edge and cloud security share common objectives of protecting data, infrastructure, and applications, they require different approaches and solutions due to their distinct characteristics and deployment models. Organizations must implement a multi-layered security strategy that addresses the unique security challenges and considerations of both edge and cloud computing environments.

## 5.4 Ethical Implications of Edge Computing

Edge computing raises several ethical implications that need to be carefully considered to ensure responsible and equitable deployment. Here are some key ethical considerations associated with edge computing:

## 1. Data Privacy and Consent:

- Edge computing involves processing and storing data closer to the source, which may raise concerns about data privacy and consent.

- Organizations must ensure that individuals are informed about the collection, processing, and use of their data and obtain explicit consent when required by law or regulations.

## 2. Bias and Fairness:

- Algorithms deployed at the edge may perpetuate biases or discrimination if they are trained on biased datasets or reflect the biases of their developers.

- Ensuring fairness and accountability in edge computing systems requires transparent and unbiased data collection, algorithmic decision-making, and regular audits to detect and mitigate bias.

### *3. Accessibility and Digital Divide:*

- Edge computing technologies may exacerbate the digital divide by widening the gap between those who have access to high-speed internet and computing resources and those who do not.

- Ensuring equitable access to edge computing infrastructure and services, especially in underserved communities, is essential to prevent further marginalization and promote digital inclusion.

### 4. Security and Trustworthiness:

- Edge devices and networks are susceptible to security threats, including malware, data breaches, and unauthorized access.

- Ensuring the security and trustworthiness of edge computing systems requires robust encryption, authentication, and access controls to protect data and infrastructure from cyberattacks and privacy breaches.

## 5. Accountability and Transparency:

- Edge computing introduces complexities in accountability and transparency, as data processing and decision-making occur closer to the source, often without visibility or oversight.

- Organizations deploying edge computing solutions must establish clear lines of accountability, transparency, and responsibility for the collection, processing, and use of data, as well as for the decisions made by edge systems.

## 6. Environmental Impact:

- Edge computing infrastructure, including edge devices and data centers, consumes energy and resources, contributing to environmental impacts such as carbon emissions and electronic waste.

- Adopting energy-efficient hardware, optimizing resource utilization, and adopting sustainable practices in the design and operation of edge computing systems can help mitigate environmental impacts.

## 7. Governance and Regulation:

+ Edge computing introduces challenges in governance and regulation, as data processing and decision-making occur across distributed and heterogeneous environments.

+ Governments and regulatory bodies must adapt existing laws and regulations to address the unique challenges posed by edge computing, including data privacy, security, and accountability.

Addressing these ethical implications requires a multidisciplinary approach that involves collaboration among stakeholders, including technology developers, policymakers, ethicists, and civil society organizations. By adopting ethical principles and best practices, organizations can ensure that edge computing technologies are deployed responsibly and in ways that benefit society while minimizing harm and promoting equity and justice.

## 5.5 Regulatory Frameworks and Best Practices

Regulatory frameworks and best practices are crucial for ensuring the responsible and ethical deployment of edge computing technologies. Here are some key regulatory frameworks and best practices relevant to edge computing:

### *1. Data Protection and Privacy Regulations:*

- Regulations like the General Data Protection Regulation (GDPR) in the European Union and the California Consumer Privacy Act (CCPA) in the United States govern the collection, processing, and storage of personal data.

- Organizations deploying edge computing solutions must comply with these regulations by implementing data protection measures, obtaining consent for data processing, and ensuring the security of personal information.

### *2. Cybersecurity Standards and Regulations:*

- Standards such as ISO/IEC 27001 and regulatory frameworks like the NIST Cybersecurity Framework provide guidance on managing cybersecurity risks and protecting data and systems from cyber threats.

- Organizations should implement robust cybersecurity measures, including encryption, access controls, and regular security assessments, to safeguard edge computing infrastructure and data.

## 3. Industry-Specific Regulations:

+ Certain industries, such as healthcare (e.g., HIPAA) and finance (e.g., PCI DSS), have specific regulatory requirements for data protection and security.

+ Organizations deploying edge computing solutions in regulated industries must ensure compliance with industry-specific regulations to protect sensitive information and maintain trust with customers.

## 4. Ethical Guidelines and Principles:

+ Ethical guidelines, such as those outlined in the IEEE Ethically Aligned Design and the ACM Code of Ethics, provide principles for responsible technology development and deployment.

+ Organizations should consider ethical implications such as fairness, transparency, accountability, and privacy when designing and implementing edge computing systems.

## 5. Transparency and Accountability:

- Transparency and accountability are essential for building trust with stakeholders and ensuring responsible deployment of edge computing technologies.
- Organizations should be transparent about their data practices, security measures, and how edge computing systems are used, and they should be accountable for any potential risks or harms.

## 6. Cross-Border Data Transfer Regulations:

- Cross-border data transfer regulations, such as the EU-US Privacy Shield and Standard Contractual Clauses, govern the transfer of personal data between different jurisdictions.
- Organizations must ensure compliance with these regulations when transferring data across borders in their edge computing deployments.

## 7. Regular Audits and Assessments:

- Regular audits and assessments of edge computing systems help ensure compliance with regulatory requirements and identify potential security vulnerabilities or areas for improvement.

- Organizations should conduct periodic audits and
  assessments of their edge computing infrastructure,
  data practices, and security controls to maintain
  compliance and mitigate risks.

### *8. Collaboration and Information Sharing:*

- Collaboration among industry stakeholders,
  regulatory authorities, and cybersecurity experts is
  essential for addressing regulatory challenges and
  sharing best practices.

- Organizations should participate in industry forums,
  working groups, and information-sharing initiatives
  to stay informed about regulatory developments and
  emerging threats in edge computing.

By adhering to regulatory frameworks and implementing
best practices, organizations can ensure that their edge
computing deployments are compliant, secure, and ethically
sound. This not only helps mitigate legal and reputational
risks but also fosters trust with customers, partners, and the
wider community.